# Hidden Beauty
*Seeing God in Japan*

Roger W. Lowther

ISBN 978-1-953704-42-9 HARDCOVER
ISBN 978-1-953704-43-6 PAPERBACK

Cover design by Verity Hayhow
Cover image by Marc Stan/Stocksy

Community Arts Media
Tokyo, Japan
*www.communityarts.jp*
*info@communityarts.jp*

*To the artist community*
*searching with me*
*for the hidden beauty of God in Japan*

# Contents

כְּבֹד אֱלֹהִים הַסְתֵּר דָּבָר
וּכְבֹד מְלָכִים חֲקֹר דָּבָר׃

It is the glory of God to conceal his speech,

and the glory of kings to search it out.

PROVERBS 25:2 (translation by author)

*Foreword by Toshiyuki Machida*

## VISIBLE ART AND THE INVISIBLE GOD

I became a Christian in art school. My friend's natural artistic ability made me extremely jealous, and when I attended a church service for the first time at the invitation of the English professor, who was an American missionary, I not only saw the sin of my jealousy but a way to heal from it. Through the words of the Bible, I accepted Jesus Christ as my Lord and Savior.

I had never met another Japanese Christian before and thought I was the very first one! Two maps came to mind. The first, a map of the world showing how the gospel traveled for 2,000 years until it finally reached me. The second, a map of Japan showing where I now had to carry it to.

However, I had a problem with being both an artist and a Christian. God is invisible, but art is visible. This dualistic line of thinking about visible art and the invisible God made me lose all motivation for painting. Despite the certainty of my salvation, I despaired.

I finished degrees in art from college and graduate school, worked at a design firm for a couple of years, studied at seminary, and then served as a pastor for 11 years.

I met with a couple from a nearby church who also was interested in art and troubled by the seeming lack of connection between art and God. Though music is often found in the church, art is rarely discussed for fear of becoming an idol, perhaps as a response to the Reformation. As we studied the Bible together looking for themes of "art," I learned more about the beauty of God's visible world and how God himself directed the designs of the tabernacle and temple. I came to understand that God and art are deeply connected.

When Jesus said, "Look at the birds of the air" (Matthew 6:26), he taught about the invisible kingdom of God through visible things. He showed that the visible and the invisible do not contradict one another and that he himself is the invisible become visible. We can do art because Jesus embodies both.

> "No one has ever seen God; the only God, who is at
> the Father's side, he has made him known." (John 1:18,
> ESV)

Twenty-two years after becoming a Christian, I established Bible & Art Ministries (B&A),[1] a mission organization designed to spread the gospel through the arts. B&A shows the connection of God with art and helps artists who want to witness their love for Jesus through their artwork.

I first met Roger about 10 years ago, when he came to a talk I gave on paintings with biblical themes. He also attended one of our large exhibitions. In turn, I attended some of his events, where Roger and his team witness the gospel not only through visual arts but through all areas of human creativity.

I wish I could have read this book when I first became a Christian. Though that was not possible, it is now possible for all of us. Through his artistic sensibilities and love for the Japanese people, Roger brings fresh insights into how God truly reveals his

---

1 *https://bibleandart.jimdofree.com/*

beauty in Japan. Through this book, I pray that many more people will discover God's deep connection to their lives and that their love for the Lord Jesus would continue to increase in passion for him.

Toshiyuki Machida
director, *Bible & Art Ministries*
*Tokyo, Japan*

*Introduction*

**I OFTEN GLIMPSE BEAUTY** in Japanese art in the silent spaces between objects, brush strokes, and sound. In the fall of 2017, we hosted the "Hidden Beauty" Art Festival in downtown Tokyo,[1] celebrating various Japanese traditional arts around the theme of hidden beauty: *sumie* ink painting, where white space is as important as strokes on the paper, *ikebana* flower arranging, where space between flowers and twigs communicates as powerfully as the objects themselves, music of the Japanese *koto*, where silence is performed as well as sound, and artwork by Japan's "Hidden" Christians, where references to Christ, Mary, the cross, and the apostles are covered or concealed in symbolism.

---

1 Community Arts Tokyo and Grace City Church Tokyo sponsored this event at Hamarikyu Asahi Hall in Tokyo on October 14, 2017. In Japanese, the festival was called " 隠れた 美 " (*kakureta bi*).

I encounter another hidden beauty as well, the beauty of the God of the Bible. Though many in Japan view Christianity as an "outside" foreign religion, God revealed his glory and presence in Japan long before those first missionaries stepped off boats in the 16th century.

In my other books, I explored how God speaks through Japanese art and culture. *The Broken Leaf* meditates on pointers to the gospel found in Japanese traditional arts such as *kintsugi* pottery repair, *urushi* lacquer techniques, the music of the *koto*, and the incense ceremony. *Aroma of Beauty*[3] explores the presence of God in the midst of the March 11, 2011 earthquake in Japan, and *A Taste of Grace*[4] shows how God shares his love with us through the food we eat every day in Japan. This book, *Hidden Beauty*, can be considered fourth in the series with meditations on the echoes of the voice of God who speaks through all things, including the art and culture of Japan.

2  Roger W. Lowther, *The Broken Leaf: Meditations on Art, Life, and Faith in Japan*. Eugene, OR: Wipf & Stock, 2009.

3  Roger W. Lowther, *Aroma of Beauty in the Wake of the 2011 Tsunami in Japan*. Boston: Community Arts Media, 2021.

4  Roger W. Lowther, *A Taste of Grace*. Boston: Community Arts Media, 2024.

I find deep meaning in the Japanese verb *tsukuru* 造る ("to make"), which has two parts. The radical on the left (辶) means "path or proceed forward," and the part on the right (告) means "tell, inform, or announce." Together, they form the character (造), which I take to have the nuance of "information proceeding forth." When I first learned this character, my eyes were drawn to the part in the bottom that looks like a square (口) which means "mouth" as learned by every first-year Japanese language student. Many words related to communication contain this character: 言う ("to say"), 話す ("to speak"), 語る ("to tell"), 喋る ("to talk"). All of creation—everything that has been made and will ever be made—communicates "information that proceeds forward" from the mouth of God.

Many pastors in Japan refer to the God of the Bible as the Creator Lord God, maker (造) of heaven and earth, because this sets him apart from the *Yaoyorozu no Kami*, the eight million gods of the Shinto religion. Only the Creator Lord God has the power to send forth his information and declare his glory through all creation.

"The heavens *declare* the glory of God;
the skies *proclaim* the work of his hands.
Day after day they pour forth *speech*;
night after night they *reveal* knowledge.
They have no speech, they use no words;
no sound is heard from them.
Yet their *voice* goes out into all the earth,
their *words* to the ends of the world." (Psalm 19:1–4)

God's voice declares, proclaims, speaks, reveals, and goes out to the ends of the world through creation into every nation, tribe, and people, including the nation of Japan. Verse 4 of this psalm in particular reminds me of Japan, long considered the end of the world as the eastern terminus of the historic Silk Road. Though we cannot always hear it with our ears, the message of God is hidden in all things made because we live in a universe literally saturated with the voice of God.[5]

---

5 Pierce Taylor Hibbs writes, "Every speck of material is covered with an ancient and holy conversation, through which it has come into being," and "Because all things are essentially linguistic products of the Trinitarian God and mark his presence in the world, there is a sense in which God has written himself in everything." *God of Words: Essays on God and Language* (2022) 182, 264.

"For since the creation of the world God's invisible qualities—his eternal power and divine nature—have been clearly seen, being understood from what has been made." (Romans 1:20)

Invisible yet clearly seen, pointers to God pour forth through all things. Day after day and night after night, they reveal knowledge of his glory. As we discover together the hidden beauty of God in Japan, may we draw closer in worship of him. In so doing, we fulfill the very thing we were made (造) to do.[6]

---

6 *The Westminster Shorter Catechism* (1647): "Q1. What is the chief end of man? A. Man's chief end is to glorify God, and to enjoy him forever."

# I.
## Hidden Beauty

We fix our eyes
not on what is seen,
but on what is unseen.
2 CORINTHIANS 4:18

**A COUPLE OF HOUR'S** train ride west of Tokyo, I enter the Miki Sawada Memorial Museum, which displays one of the biggest collections in the world of objects made by "Hidden Christians." During a time of severe persecution in the early 1600s, Christians had to keep their faith secret or face certain death, not only for themselves but for every member of their *gonin gumi* (group of five families). In an effort to increase pressure and manipulate loyalty in Japanese society, the government divided everyone into small groups of families to keep an eye on each other. If they found even one Christian, they would kill them all, children and elderly alike.

As I slowly stroll up and down each aisle, I see wooden statues of all sizes that look like the bodhisattva holding a child. They do not appear to have anything to do with Christianity, but the artists have hidden images of Jesus on the cross in a back panel or under the base. These "Maria Kannon" statues gave men and women a physical way to secretly worship Jesus and feel his presence as they appeared to recite Buddhist prayers.

I see metal sword guards of all shapes and sizes. One shows fishermen with their nets to symbolize the disciples of Jesus. Another shows Christ on the cross, only visible when the hand guard is removed from the sword. The bearer of the sword secretly held these reminders of the presence of Jesus everywhere they carried it.

I see an intricately carved household shrine with the cross hidden in the back of a man and under movable panels.[1] I pass stone lanterns with images

---

1 A picture of this *zushi* shrine can be seen on the museum's

of the cross carved at the base, below where it would normally be covered with dirt and plants. I marvel at a bronze mirror that displays an image of Jesus on the cross on the wall when light reflects off of it.

The artists made these objects at incredible risk to their own lives and the lives of their families and neighbors. But with deep faith, they carefully etched traces of Jesus's sacrifice into ordinary objects that could be safely displayed in homes. Only a few could see their marvelous skill. Hidden beauty infused the objects with hidden meaning. The secret nature did not take away from the beauty, but, if anything, enhanced it.

My thoughts drift to all the gorgeous artwork God had artisans make for the inner room of his tabernacle and temple. These hidden parts were for the eyes of the High Priest and God alone. The rest of Israel never saw these objects made with their Spirit-filled craftsmanship and beauty. What does this hidden beauty tell us about God and what we are waiting to behold?

_____

website: *https://www.elizabeth-sh.jp/memorialmuseum/collection/view/91.*

I thank God that we can now openly worship God in Japan, as I celebrate the work of these artists who prayed that this day would one day come.

1. Many Christians decorate their homes with images of the cross. Can you imagine having to hide those images?

2. What do you think the hidden beauty of the tabernacle tells us about God and what we are waiting to behold?

# II.
## 50 Martyrs and 47 Ronin

God demonstrated
His own love for us in this:
While we were still sinners,
Christ [the Lord] died for us.
ROMANS 5:8

## 50 MARTYRS

On December 4, 1623, 50 followers of Christ were marched from the center of Edo Tokyo to a hill just outside the city gate, where they were bound to wooden poles and burned alive. On Christmas Day, the authorities repeated this horrific act for 37 others, wives and children of the previous martyrs and those who gave them shelter.[1] One of the largest

---

1 *http://www.stutler.cc/russ/kirishitan.html*. Accessed April 19,

public executions of Christians in Japanese history, this atrocity put their faith and loyalty to God on full display.

On a cold winter morning almost 400 years later, I followed their path with a group of Japanese Christian leaders and pastors. Snow blew in our faces as we endured the strong winds rushing between the rows of skyscrapers that now line the streets of central Tokyo. Each of us held a piece of paper with the name of one martyr from that day. Mine read "Peter" Shozaburo. Who was this man? What was his story? I know nothing about him but his name.

After an eight-hour walk, we approached the end of their journey in what is now the bustling train station of Shinagawa, following noisy railroad tracks of what used to be the coastline of Tokyo Bay. My body shivered. My feet ached. How much worse it must have been for the men on that day centuries earlier! Only one large foundation of stone remained of the ancient city gate. Only a small memorial stone hidden in the shadow of a large office building remained of the former martyrs' hill.

---

2023.

## 47 *RONIN*

Mere minutes away on another hilltop, the famous temple of Sengakuji marks the end of another historic march. On January 31, 1703, 47 *ronin* samurai with no master traversed heavy snows from the city's center following the very same road as the martyrs, carrying the decapitated head of their enemy in a bucket! Their vengeance for the death of their master became known as the Ako Incident. To atone for their crime, by order of the shogun, they committed *seppuku* death by a self-inflicted stab to their stomachs and were buried there at the temple. Today, businessmen and women continue to visit their graves and honor them for their loyalty to their master to the point of death.

Walking through the cold winter wind, I thought about these two groups of men, the 50 martyrs and the 47 *ronin*. Both marched to the edge of the city to show loyalty to their master. Both climbed a hill to their place of execution. The 50 martyrs, all but forgotten to the general public but gaining eternal life with their master, and the 47 *ronin,* continuously immortalized in movies, books, and art.[2] The 50 followers of Christ

---

2  The group of men who stayed behind at the Fukushima Daiichi

marched for their heavenly Lord. The 47 *ronin* for their earthly lord.

## ONE LORD OF ALL

Walking that road, I thought about all the similarities and differences to the death of Jesus Christ. He, too, marched through the city and up a hill to his place of execution. He, too, was publicly displayed as a criminal. The crime of the *ronin* was murder. The crime of the martyrs was faith. The only crime of Jesus was love. The martyrs and *ronin* gave their lives for their master above them, but Jesus gave his life for the sinners beneath him. We should be serving Jesus, but Jesus instead served us.

> "[He] emptied himself, by taking the form of a servant. . . . He humbled himself by becoming [loyal] to the point of death, even death on a cross." (Philippians 2:7–8)

The loyalty of the Son of God changes lives, because he personally walked that path at the penalty

---

Nuclear Power Plant to prevent further disaster were dubbed the "Fukushima 50" by the media. They were being compared to the 47 *ronin*, sacrificing their lives to regain lost honor.

of death, in order to open the path of eternal life for us.

1. What comes to mind when you think of loyalty?
2. Has anyone ever shown loyalty to you?
3. How far should loyalty go? Should it be to the point of death?

# III.
## *Perceiving the Sound*

> Blessed are the people
> who know the joyful sound!
> They walk, O Lord,
> in the light of Your countenance.
> PSALM 89:15 (NKJV)

**ON LONGER RUNS UP THE RIVER** from my apartment building, I come to Sensoji Temple, the oldest temple in Tokyo. According to legend, Kannon appeared as a gold statue to two brothers fishing in 628 A.D. They tried multiple times to return the statue to the river, but it continued to pursue them. Eventually, the chief of the village decided to turn his home into a shrine so that everyone could come and worship there.

Today around Sensoji, I see signs everywhere for

Kannon ( 観音 ), which literally means "see sound." Kannon, the Bodhisattva of compassion and mercy, sees and listens to all sounds of suffering. Some statues display eleven heads to be aware of all suffering, a "thousand" eyes to see all suffering, and a "thousand" arms to reach out and relieve all suffering. Though able to achieve the peace of Nirvana, Kannon is "The Merciful One" who waits with compassion for all suffering beings.

During the roughly two hundred and fifty years of persecution in Japan, "Hidden Christians" used images and statues of Kannon to secretly worship the God of the Bible. Sometimes, they made the statues look like the Virgin Mary holding baby Jesus, what are known as "Maria Kannon." Sometimes, they simply hid a cross in the back or the base.

It's fascinating to think about Jesus in a culture where Kannon is so prevalent. Jesus is the greatest of all perceivers. He is the One who sees and hears all our cries of pain and suffering.

> "The eyes of the LORD are on the righteous, and his ears are attentive to their cry. . . . The righteous cry out, and the LORD hears them; he delivers them from

all their troubles." (Psalm 34:15, 17)

Jesus is the greatest of all merciful ones, who reaches out with his mighty arm to save.

> "The arm of the LORD is not too short to save, nor his ear too dull to hear" (Isaiah 59:1)

More than a reappearing statue, Jesus is the greatest of all pursuers, "the Hound of Heaven,"[1] who never stops until he has brought peace to people from every language, tribe, and nation.

> "Here I am! I stand at the door and knock." (Revelation 3:20)

Jesus the merciful Savior "sees all sound" of our cries of pain and suffering and answers with his own cries of pain and suffering from the cross. Jesus responds to our cries for mercy with the "blessed sound," the *fukuin* ( 福音 ) of the gospel.

---

1 A poem by Francis Thompson (1859–1907) that portrays God as relentlessly pursuing his people. *http://www.houndofheaven.com/poem.*

1.  What do you consider examples of "blessed sound"?

2.  How does the Bible passage, "The arm of the LORD is not too short to save, nor his ear too dull to hear" (Isaiah 59:1), bring comfort in suffering?

3.  In the original Greek, gospel means "good news." What is the good news? How is the Japanese translation as "blessed sound" different?

4.  How does Jesus's pursuit of us to not only relieve suffering but have a relationship with us ("walk . . . in the light of thy countenance") make his message more powerful?

# IV.
## *Wrestling for a Blessing*

Jacob was left alone,
and a man wrestled
with him till daybreak.
GENESIS 32:24

**IN THE TRADITIONAL JAPANESE SPORT** of *sumo*, two practically naked men wrestle each other to the ground or out of the ring. The center for *sumo* lies just up the river from where I live, in Ryogoku, where I often see these large athletes on the streets dressed in their traditional garments and sandals.

The Japanese word for *sumo* wrestlers is *rikishi* ( 力士 ). The first character, *riki* (力), means "strong," and the second, *shi* (士), means "warrior." These "strong warriors" face off in the wrestling ring, while making one imagine some kind of larger significance in their hand-to-hand struggle.

*Sumo* started around 700 A.D. as a ritual dance to wrestle for a blessing from the gods. Many of those religious elements remain today. What looks like the top of a shrine covers the *dohyo* ring, a place frequently prayed over. Wrestlers sip sacred water, purify the ring with salt, stomp their feet to ward off evil spirits, and clap their hands to call the attention of the gods. Sparse attire prevents grabbing and concealing weapons, but, more importantly, symbolizes spiritual nakedness. Even the *mawashi* loincloth reminds one of the sacred ropes that hang on Shinto shrines and trees.

Every year, professional *sumo* wrestlers visit my sons' kindergarten to visit with the students and beat *mochi*, a kind of rice cake. They pick up large, heavy wooden mallets and pound the rice over and over again. At the end of the day, the children usually hang from the arms and legs of the wrestlers, some of whom weigh over 400 lbs. The only way a massive man like that can safely interact with the children is to hold back his weight and strength. He takes special care not to accidentally step or lean on any of the small humans excitedly attacking him.

*Sumo* reminds me of the most important event in Jacob's life from the Bible. He received his name, which means "wrestling" or "grappling," after he grabbed his brother's heel at birth. He then spent a lifetime fighting with his family members.

Jacob stole his father's blessing when he was young and ran away from home. He lived decades in a far-off land before heading back home full of anxiety, when a mysterious stranger appeared in the dark and wrestled him until morning. At sunrise, this stranger tapped Jacob's tendon at the hip, tearing it and crippling him for the rest of his life. I am told this tendon is the strongest in the human body, virtually impossible to tear with human strength.[1]

When Jacob realized this man was God, he grabbed onto him and, in his agony and awe, cried out, "I will not let you go unless you bless me" (Genesis 32:26). Jacob then received a blessing and a new name, Israel, which means, "one who struggles with God."

"Your name will no longer be Jacob, but Israel,

1 Ann Voskamp, *One Thousand Gifts: A Dare to Live Fully Right Where You Are*. (Grand Rapids: Zondervan, 2010) 138.

because you have *struggled with God* and with humans and have overcome." (Genesis 32:28)[2]

In the turmoil of Jacob's agony and fear, God appeared and broke through his walls. Jacob realized he had not only been fighting with men but "jacobing" with God his entire life. Then he finally met God and, in his weakness, found a whole new beginning.

The writer of Hebrews asserts that Jacob accomplished his greatest act of faith by leaning on the top of his staff when he blessed his grandsons. Jacob exhibited strength not as a moral leader but as a limping and broken man. The Bible shows Jacob remembering his weakness and worshiping God through it.

> "By faith Jacob, when he was dying, blessed each of Joseph's sons, and worshiped as he leaned on the top of his staff." (Hebrews 11:21)

In the people of Israel, God built a family who, in their weakness, rely on God alone for his presence and

---

2 See also Hosea 12:3–4, "In the womb he grasped his brother's heel; as a man he *struggled* with God. He *struggled* with the angel and overcame him; he wept and begged for his favor."

blessing.

I find one point, though, especially hard to swallow about this account of Jacob's life: Jacob seems to have not only met God in his own weakness but in God's weakness as well.

> "The man saw that he could not overpower him."
> (Genesis 32:25)

But what a strange thing to say! Why could God not overpower a mere human? The Bible emphasizes this point a few verses later.

> "You have struggled with God . . . and have overcome." (Genesis 32:28)

Did Jacob really win? God defeated him with only a light touch to the hip. The only possible way Jacob could have won is if God held back his weight and strength. God made himself weak—so weak, in fact, that he could not even overpower Jacob. And through the weakness of God, Jacob was victorious. Like the *sumo* wrestlers with children at my son's kindergarten, God held back because Jacob could only meet God in

God's weakness.

Jacob's injury in the hip also symbolically refers to his loins and offspring. By smiting Jacob on the hip, God was smiting the offspring of Jacob. What an amazing pointer to Jesus as the true offspring of Jacob! When the woman at the well asked Jesus, "Are you greater than our father Jacob?" Jesus responded that indeed he was (John 4:14).

The wrestling of Jacob points to Jesus's defeat in weakness as our triumph. Through Christ's loss, we have victory. The full weight of God's judgment fell on Christ on the cross so that only a small part of this judgment would fall on us. The full strength of God's wrath fell on Christ on the cross so that only a small part of this wrath would fall on us. Jesus took the ultimate blow of justice so that we may receive the smaller blows of his love.

> *A tearing of the thigh for an opening of the eye.*[3] . . .
> *Only those who limp know how to see.*[4]

Jacob held on and lived through the pain for the

---

3  Ibid, 139.

4  Ibid, 140.

full blessing of God. On the cross, Jesus held on and died for the full blessing of God, not for his own sake but for ours. God cursed the one who deserved the blessing so that we would get the blessing instead of the curse. "All peoples on earth will be blessed through you and your offspring" (Genesis 28:14), God told Jacob. Through Jacob's Offspring (with a capital O), we, too, receive the inheritance of this blessing.

Christ entered the ultimate *dohyo* ring to fight the battle no one else could fight. Christ endured the full weight and strength no one else could endure. Christ, the ultimate *rikishi*, the ultimate strong man, became our champion by fighting in weakness. Our glory comes through weakness perfected by our ultimate champion.[5]

---

5 I am thinking particularly of *yokozuna* wrestlers who achieve the highest rank and are the living embodiment of *sumo*.

1.  How have you seen an opponent become weak in order to win in another kind of way?

2.  How do athletes represent others in sports events? What else do they represent?

3.  What does it mean for Jesus to be the "champion" of our faith?

# V.
## *Gathered Together*

For you created my inmost being;
you knit me together
in my mother's womb.
I praise you because
I am fearfully and wonderfully made;
your works are wonderful,
I know that full well.
My frame was not hidden from you
when I was made in the secret place,
when I was woven together
in the depths of the earth.
PSALM 139:13–15

**"I MADE THIS PIECE JUST LAST WEEK."**

Mona passes me a narrow bracelet, tightly braided

with sixteen strands of very thin copper wire.

"Take a look at this one too. It's a bit more complicated, made from forty-eight wires."

The bracelet, silver this time, lies heavy in my hands. A thick piece of metal and hook secure each end to join it together. The black of the inner sections of the braid contrast beautifully with the sparkling silver of the outer parts.

Mona makes jewelry through the ancient art of *kumihimo* Japanese weaving. *Kumihimo*, meaning "gathered threads," came from China in the seventh century along with Buddhism as an important technique for decorating temples. Later, it developed into various techniques for making and decorating the armor of samurai and their horses. Today, this technique often fastens the *obi* waistband of *kimono* dresses.

Looking at Mona's jewelry, I think about the community of the church. God gathers people together from every language, tribe, and nation to make one beautifully woven tapestry. A weak single thread becomes remarkably strong when woven with other threads.

"A cord of three strands is not quickly broken." (Ecclesiastes 4:12)

In some mysteriously profound way, the community of the church is "knit together in love" (Colossians 2:2, ESV) to reveal the gospel to a world unraveled in sin. The church perseveres through persecution, famine, and sword, generation after generation. The gathered church reveals its beauty and strength in each time and place with unique characteristics woven into their own local communities.

Mona's art of *kumihimo* also inspires me to think about Christ. A propane torch brings out the rich patina of color on the jewelry, and rubbed liver of sulfur gives the appearance of age and distress. The "suffering" of the jewelry makes the pieces more relatable and desirable than before with its anguished beauty. Christ brings worth out of wounds and hope out of distress. He promises that even the most damaged and tarnished soul will be transformed into a masterpiece of exquisite beauty in his skilled and scarred hands. This ultimate Artist took on human scars and experience and became isolated in order to gather together and weave his people into patterns of beautiful community.

May more and more people be braided into this glorious throng in worship.[1]

---

1 You can see pictures of Mona's jewelry and order them online at *www.monas-musings.com*.

1.  *Kumihimo* is made from gathering single strands into one beautiful piece. What symbolism do you see in that?

2.  What are examples of "isolated and broken strands" in our broken world?

3.  How is the community of the church practically "knit together in love"?

# VI.
## An Obi of Love

And over all these virtues
put on love,
which binds them all together
in perfect unity.
COLOSSIANS 3:14

**MANY VARIETIES OF *OBI* SASHES** complement
Japanese traditional clothing. They can be wide
or narrow, simple or ornate, cheap or expensive.
Some outweigh the worth of all the rest of the outfit
combined. But no matter how complex the *kimono*
or other parts of the Japanese outfit, the *obi* holds all
the layers together. Without it, the garment remains
unfinished.

"Clothe yourselves with compassion, kindness,

> humility, gentleness and patience. . . . Over all these
> virtues put on love, which binds them all together in
> perfect unity." (Colossians 3:12, 14)

The Japanese Bible translates this phrase "binds them all together" as "bound with an *obi*."[1] The Bible compares love to an *obi* that can be wrapped around us, holding together all other spiritual characteristics. Just like each layer of the *kimono*, each spiritual virtue shines in beauty, but we still need an *obi* of love to bring them to completion. With the binding power of love, all virtues come to fruition.

The love God pours out for us far exceeds the love we give one another. In the beginning, we unsuccessfully tried to cover ourselves with fig leaves. Then God made beautiful garments of animal skins. The garments covered us, protected us, and gave us a safety and beauty surpassing what we had before, shadows of the garments the Son of God will one day wrap us with, perfectly bound with the *obi* of God's love.

What a beautiful picture of what God has

---

1 Deane Schuessler, *Devoted to God and to Each Other*. (Enumclaw, WA: WinePress Publishing, 2006) 97–98.

accomplished! May we all be bound with the Japanese *obi* of God's love and see ourselves and others as God sees us. We finally find completion when clothed in the beautiful garments of God and perfectly bound in his love.

1. Have you ever worn a *kimono* or an *obi*? What was the occasion?

2. Does a *kimono* or *obi* hold any special memories for you?

3. The Apostle Paul wrote the following, "Stand firm then, with the belt of truth buckled around your waist" (Ephesians 6:14). How is this image of the belt of truth different from the Japanese image of the *obi* of love?

4. Do any other items of clothing we wear symbolize the love of God?

# VII.
## Sound of Cloth

"Blessed is the one who stays awake
and remains clothed,
so as not to go naked
and be shamefully exposed."

REVELATION 16:15

**"YOU NEED SOMETHING BETTER** for your concerts," Kei tells me, a fashion designer who recently became a Christian.

As an organist, I usually wear a black tux in concerts, which admittedly is completely plain on the back, the only part audiences can see during the performance. "Will you make something for me?" I ask.

"Of course!" he says.

Kei and I meet up the very next week to pick out materials from a fabric store: red and gold braided thread, black cords, and . . . feathers! He combines these with his grandmother's old black and white *kimono*, creating especially intricate designs, cuts, and layers on the back. The finished product is far from boring, full of celebratory majesty fit for the most extravagant of concerts.

Not long after, Kei founded *Sound of Cloth*[1] to explore the relationships between humanity and the natural world. We can flourish only because of the various coverings and protections that shield us. Kei brings these invisible forms of protection to our attention by making them visible through fashion. Through making clothes, he asks, "What good things does creation give us? How does it surround and protect us?" The atmosphere protects us from deadly radiation and the cold expanse of space. Plants quietly remove harmful gases and provide oxygen for us to breathe. Fabric and skins made from plants and animals wrap our bodies to protect us from the wind

---

1 You can learn more about Sound of Cloth at *www.soundofcloth. com*.

and cold.

One of Kei's lines of clothing works with cloth cut to the shape of mushrooms. Rather than symmetrically streamlining it to the human body, he playfully brings out the irregular shapes and curves in the material. He finds beauty in the creative sense of balance like that found in *ikebana* flower arrangements. As mushrooms depend on hosts to thrive and grow, this clothing also symbolically portrays its deep dependence on family, friends, and community to flourish by incorporating repurposed materials.

His seaweed line began after the Great East Japan Earthquake in 2011, when Japan faced a global crisis. The broken Fukushima Nuclear Power Plants released deadly amounts of radioactivity into the air and sea, destroying the farming and fishing industries. Many lost their livelihoods and turned to growing seaweed and flax instead. Kei cuts and sews Fukushima-made linen into amorphous shapes that reflect the enlarged cellular structures of seaweed. These clothes reflect the ability of seaweed to protect the body from the intake of radioactive isotopes by flooding it with natural iodine.

Kei has also explored the symbiosis of man with bacteria, yeast, silicon, and butterflies. His fig leaf line uses large pieces of expensive, gold-colored silk in the shape of fig leaves, alluding to the first clothing mentioned in the Bible.

> "The eyes of both of them were opened, and they realized they were naked; so they sewed fig leaves together and made coverings for themselves." (Genesis 3:7)

Themes of wrapping, surrounding, and protecting abound in the Bible. Through making clothing, Kei consciously participates in God's work of covering people. Right after the fall, God gave Adam and Eve clothing from animal skin to physically and symbolically cover and protect them.

> "The Lord God made garments of skin for Adam and his wife and clothed them." (Genesis 3:21)

By shedding the blood of animals, God showed that their covering would one day come through the shedding of the blood of Christ. "[The Lord] has clothed me with garments of salvation and arrayed me in a robe of his righteousness," writes Isaiah (61:10). "You forgave the iniquity of your people and covered all their sins," sings the psalmist (Psalm 85:2). "Cloth[e] yourselves with Christ," writes Paul (Galatians 3:27).

The name of Kei's company, *Sound of Cloth*, includes deep layers of meaning. In Japanese, the word for clothing, *fuku*, is a homonym with the word for "blessing." The gospel, *fukuin*, literally means "sound of blessing" but sounds the same as "sound of cloth." Kei brings out this "sound of blessing" by physically making the grace of God's protection visible to people through clothing.

Through our clothes, we can celebrate the protection and salvation provided by our loving Creator. Every day, we literally wear the gospel reminders of this covering we have already received and will one day receive in perfection through Christ's shed blood on the cross.

1. Some people intentionally use clothing as a form of self-expression and not just covering and protection. How do you use your clothing?

2. How do you think Christ and the gospel are reflected in our clothing?

# VIII.
## Beautiful in His Sight

"I clothed you with an embroidered dress
and put sandals of fine leather on you.
I dressed you in fine linen
and covered you with costly garments.
I adorned you with jewelry:
I put bracelets on your arms
and a necklace around your neck,
and I put a ring on your nose,
earrings on your ears
and a beautiful crown on your head. . . .
Your fame spread among the nations
on account of your beauty,
because the splendor I had given you
made your beauty perfect,
declares the Sovereign LORD."
EZEKIEL 16:10–12, 14

**A YOUNG WOMAN JUMPS UPWARD,** hair blown by the wind. Pink rouge brings out cheeks flushed with happiness. Her blue and white dress expresses the boundless joy of sky and ocean. Sparkling confetti expresses excitement.

Another woman lies on a bed of small flowers. Pink and white makeup on the lips and around the eyes mirror the colors of the flowers, contrasting with her wavy black hair. Creases and wrinkles are wiped away, expressing comfort in the intimacy with nature.

Another young woman stands in front of a wall covered with large butterflies. Her white camisole, unmade hair, and minimal makeup together paint a picture of carefree innocence.

Each of these pictures captures the beauty of a moment by the company *La Beauté* ("Beauty").[1] Hitomi, the founder of the company, aims to bring out latent beauty in order to capture it in photographs, film, and performances. Her work as a makeup artist involves far more than the skillful use of cosmetics and hairstyling. She considers how a head tilted upward lengthens the body and stretches out face and neck

---

1  *https://at-labeaute.com/*

muscles, erasing lines of tension and stress, and how a slight breeze gives a carefree and natural aura. She matches clothing to backgrounds to express a wide range of themes and moods and combines light, wind, movement, and color to express emotions and experiences.

Foundation and rouge make the skin look young and healthy. Lipstick and liner emphasize natural contrasts in the lips, eyelashes, and eyebrows. Hair spray and wax give shape and body to the hair. Earrings and necklaces adorn the ears and neck. Nail polish and rings give color and sparkle to fingers.

Hitomi describes her work this way: "God made this world and everything in it. With the God-given building blocks of this physical world, we strive to display the beauty which only comes from God. Through the technique of making people up, *La Beauté* endeavors to gift the human heart with the fleeting and momentary beauty of this world." Beauty of people on earth hints to us of the splendor of those in heaven as God will one day remake them to be.

God beautifully and lavishly dresses and decorates his people with adornments of fine linen, costly garments, gold, and silver. Ezekiel 16 displays this inner and outer loveliness that comes from God, a beauty that grows in splendor through relationship with God.

> "The splendor I had given you made your beauty perfect, declares the Sovereign LORD." (Ezeziel 16:14)

God makes us beautiful in his eyes and adorns us with "splendor" to perfect that glory. We are honored with great worth in his eyes (Isaiah 43:4). The charm he now gives will last for an eternity in heaven.

> "I saw the Holy City, the new Jerusalem, coming down out of heaven from God, prepared as a bride beautifully dressed for her husband." (Revelation 21:2)

Truly, we are ravishingly beautiful in the eyes of God. With this kind of love that banishes all insecurity, God gifts us with more freedom, joy, and fulfillment than we could ever hope for or imagine.

1. What do you think about how makeup is used in your culture?

2. What does it mean that God perfects our beauty with the splendor he gives us?

3. How would it affect you if you truly believed you were ravishingly beautiful in the eyes of God?

# IX.
## Snapshots and Watching Eyes

Let us run with perseverance
the race marked out for us,
fixing our eyes on Jesus,
the pioneer and perfecter of faith.

HEBREWS 12:1–2

**I AM GREETED BY A DISTURBING POSTER** every time I enter the bicycle parking at the base of my building. Drawn in the *kabuki* style, thick red, white, and black eyeliner surrounds terrible eyes on a bright yellow face. Words read, "Someone is watching you!" Variations of this poster appear quite frequently around the city of Tokyo, terrorizing the masses into obeying the rules.

I don't know whether or not this poster fulfills

its purpose, but watching eyes don't always have to be such a terrible thing. Consider the Japanese word for "parent" (親), a combination of the characters for "stand" (立) in the upper left, "tree" (木) in the lower left, and "watch" (見) on the right. The word seems to hold the meaning "stand next to the tree and watch," something a parent might do to protect a playing child, ready to jump into action if help is needed.

Hiro, a photographer friend of mine, similarly watches the world with his camera, ready to take a snapshot at a moment's notice. He showed me how he brings the camera to his eye with lightning speed to capture a moment before he has time to process it. "Snapshots are interesting," he explains. "They tell a story and make you want to know more."

Hiro's pictures usually focus on people doing ordinary things: waiting at a bus stop, talking on a phone, or walking down the street. Usually when we see such scenes, we do not take any notice. But by the act of taking a snapshot and displaying it in a gallery, the photographer extracts hidden meaning and importance from the mundane and commonplace. His watchful art makes us stop and see the world with fresh eyes.

In the same way the artist spotlights the mundane, I think of how God, the ultimate watcher, intimately knows us. In the book of Genesis, a young, pregnant slave girl named Hagar fled persecution from her abusive mistress, Sarai. Abandoned and alone, Hagar thought no one saw her suffering. Then God spoke to her, and Hagar responded, "You are the God who sees me."

> "I have now seen the One who sees me." (Genesis 16:13)

Hagar's life was transformed through being seen by "the One who sees me."

Jesus, in calling the disciples, transforms Nathanael's life in a similar way.

> "When Jesus saw Nathanael approaching, he said of him, 'Here truly is an Israelite in whom there is no deceit.' 'How do you know me?' Nathanael asked. Jesus answered, 'I saw you while you were still under the fig tree.'" (John 1:47–48)

The eternal God observes with eternally watchful

eyes, assuring us we are seen and loved. His "snapshots" capture our lives with his kingdom perspective and give moments of our lives eternal value and worth.

As I ponder this other more pleasant meaning of "someone watching" and "standing next to the tree" in the word for parent, I also cannot help but think about the relationship of Jesus and his Father. On the tree of the cross, Jesus lost the loving gaze of his Father so that *we* may know the loving gaze of the Father. God turned his parent's eye away from his son so that he could turn his eye toward us.

Let's then "[fix] our eyes on Jesus" (Hebrews 12:2) in return for his fixed gaze on us and be utterly transformed by his love.

1. How do you feel about the notion of someone watching you?

2. Does the idea of God watching give you comfort or anxiety? If anxiety, how can you reconcile this with the responses of Hagar and Nathaniel?

# X.
## *Umbrella Community*

"Do not be afraid;
you will not be put to shame.
Do not fear disgrace;
you will not be humiliated."

ISAIAH 54:4

**ONE HUNDRED JAPANESE *WAGASA***
umbrellas made from paper and bamboo filled my
friend's *UNFOLDING* art exhibit in downtown
Nagoya.[1] Big umbrellas and small umbrellas. Clean,
new umbrellas and faded, torn umbrellas, some with
layers of unremovable grime. Only careful and patient
unfolding could reveal their hidden beauty without

---

1 The art exhibit UNFOLDING took place at the Aichi Arts &
Cultural Center in downtown Nagoya, Japan from October
11–15, 2017.

breaking the delicate bamboo frames.

The umbrellas drew each visitor to the gallery into their stories, emphasized by up-close photographs that lined the walls. Their written comments showed their joy.

> "So many colors and designs!"

> "I was overwhelmed by the splendor of a world I've never noticed before."

> "Even a simple umbrella changes dramatically just by looking at it from a different perspective."

The artist, Peter Bakelaar, explained the meaning behind the exhibit.

> "The focus is not so much these umbrellas as our own lives. As humans we think, 'If people really knew what was in my heart, if they saw what was inside me, would they still love and accept me?' This exhibit explores those feelings.

> You open one umbrella and find some tears and holes. You open another and find many more. Both of these umbrellas have something in common. They're

broken. They're wounded. They have pain.

Our lives are the same way. We all have tears. We all have wounds. But we all have joys as well. Unless the umbrellas are open, we can't see them. Unless we share what's really in our hearts, we can't experience the joy of love and vulnerability.

The *UNFOLDING* exhibit is about connecting— connecting with people who have similar experiences and pain. It's about the beauty of a community where people can truly open up."

The *wagasa* umbrellas in the exhibit made observers grapple with the need to be lovingly embraced without hiding wounds and faults, to "unfold" in a safe place, and to exist as a community of people sharing weakness.

Such community can really exist because of Jesus on the cross. He formed a community where we abandon all need for pride and self-justification. He restored our relationship with God through all the humiliation and shame of the cross and can restore our relationships with one another as well. He was despised, abandoned, ridiculed, beaten, and killed.

His arms and legs literally "unfolded." His naked body was uncovered and splayed in vulnerability. He humbled himself in weakness so that we could find new strength.

Like the ultimate broken *wagasa* umbrella, Jesus took our tears, holes, and stains on the cross so that we can be redeemed without fear from the "closet" with all our accumulated dust and damage. He endured the cross, scorning its shame, so that we can "unfold" in community despite our imperfections and see each other as valuable, precious, and beautiful. We can forgive, and we can be forgiven. We can cherish, and we can be cherished.

God rejoices when he sees healing and restoration in this kind of umbrella community even now in its unfinished state. One day, only by the grace of God, will we be able to experience it fully.

1.  Do you have any interesting memories or experiences associated with umbrellas?

2.  What fears do you have about opening up yourself to others?

3.  What is the main purpose of an umbrella? How does that overlap with the purpose of the cross?

# XI.

## *Come Away to the Skies*

"The LORD your God . . .
will exult over you with loud singing."
ZEPHANIAH 3:17 (ESV)

**THE RHYTHMS OF THE CITY** of Tokyo abound in song. A melody echoes through the parks when it is time for children to go home at the end of the day. A melody also sounds in many places of business when closing time draws near. Songs particular to each place of business, especially supermarkets and electronic stores, fill the space rather than the background music of pop songs I am used to in the States.

I appreciate more the unique jingles for the *yaki imo* baked potato truck, *tofu* truck, *ramen* truck, bread truck, recycling truck, kerosene truck, and many others when they arrive in my neighborhood. For some reason, these melodies make me nostalgically happy, like the music of ice cream trucks in my neighborhood growing up.

Even more delightful, a unique ditty plays at each train station just before the train pulls away, each with its own special charm. Musashi Koganei Station, famous for cherry blossom viewing, plays *Sakura, Sakura* ("Cherry Blossoms"). Takadanobaba Station, birthplace of *Astro Boy*, plays his theme song for the *anime* series. Ebisu Station, home to the Yebisu beer company, plays their famous jingle. And, my favorite, the train stop for Tokyo Disneyland and Tokyo DisneySea plays "It's A Small World After All."[1]

These distinctive melodies remind me of the many short songs I wrote for my wife before we were married. Usually silly, sometimes serious, I made them personal, just for her, not meant for the ears of others, to show my love for her and to show how exceptional she is to me.

When my children were little, I wrote a lullaby for

---

1 The song has been since changed to "When Your Heart Makes A Wish," an original tune written to celebrate the 15th anniversary of Tokyo DisneySea.

them based on the words to Charles Wesley's hymn *Come Away to the Skies*, and they came to love it. Before going to sleep at night, they often begged me, "Daddy! Sing the song!"

> *Come away to the skies.*
> *My beloved, arise,*
> *And rejoice in the day thou wast born.*
> *On this festival day,*
> *Come exulting away*
> *And with singing to Zion return.* (v. 1)[2]

The song not only tells of God's love for my children, but my own love for them as well, and the fullness of joy in God's presence I hope they will always know in this world.

No melody compares to the one that will ultimately come from God himself as he sings over us.

> "The LORD your God is in your midst, a mighty one who will save; he will rejoice over you with gladness; he will quiet you by his love; he will exult over you

---

2 Charles Wesley wrote these words to celebrate the birthday of his wife on October 12, 1755. It was first published in *Hymns for Families* in 1767. Words are based on Ezekiel 16:6, Song of Songs 2:10, and Isaiah 51:11.

with loud singing." (Zephaniah 3:17, ESV)

The Bible says God will exult over us with loud singing, and, because of my experiences in Japan, I imagine this will not be the same melody for everyone. This hidden manna we receive from God (Revelation 2:17) will nourish each of us uniquely for all eternity. After riding the "train" to heaven, I imagine God standing at the platform, eager to welcome us into his city with a personal expression of his love.[3] When we enter the heavenly city full of melodies and hear the one sung just for us, we will know that we belong.

God shows his care for us more than we can ever comprehend, and we can join in as he unreservedly rejoices over us with his song of love.

> *Now with singing and praise*
> *Let us spend all the days*
> *By our heavenly Father bestowed,*
> *While his grace we receive*
> *From his bounty, and live*
> *To the honor and glory of God!* (v. 2)

---

3 Among other places in the Bible, I get this idea from the image of the "white stone with a new name" in Revelation 2:17.

1. What comes to your mind when you hear certain melodies?

2. Has anyone written or sung a song just for you? What was that like?

3. Can you imagine God rejoicing over you with gladness and exulting over you with loud singing?

4. What would it be like for everyone to be sung over with their own particular melody in heaven?

# XII.
## Old Pond—Leaping Frog

God made him who had no sin
to be sin for us,
so that in him
we might become
the righteousness of God.
2 CORINTHIANS 5:21

**I RUN ALONG THE SIDE** of the Sumida River which flows through the heart of Tokyo. Hundreds of years ago, this whole area at the mouth of Tokyo Bay often flooded, filling it with ponds and marshlands. Before all the noisy expressways and construction, the *haiku* poet Matsuo Basho lived and worked here, where a  museum now stands in his honor.

In the spring of 1686, he wrote his most famous poem here. All was silent when a splash in the pond drew his attention. He wrote:

古池や　蛙飛びこむ　水の音

*Into the old pond*
*A frog leaps*
*The sound of water*

Basho vividly captures the scene and the emotions it evokes through his contrast of sound and silence, young frog and ancient pond.[1] The empty space around the words encourage readers to use their imaginations and find the hidden beauty.

Basho's student, Takarai Kikaku, wrote another *haiku.*[2]

名月や　畳の上に　松の影

*The full harvest moon*
*On the tatami mats*

---

1 Matsuo Basho, Japan's most famous poet, lived from 1644 to 1694.

2 Takarai Kikaku lived from 1661 to 1707.

*A pine tree's shadow*

Sky contrasts with earth. The bright moon brings out crisp dark lines of the pine tree's shadow. I imagine the shadow moves gently against the stillness of the tatami mats. The harvest moon signifies the transition between summer and winter and between life and death.

Novelist Junichiro Tanizaki captures the Japanese aesthetic of beauty in contrast when he wrote, "We find beauty not in the thing itself but in the patterns of shadows, the light and the darkness, that one thing against another creates."[3]

Nowhere does the beauty of contrasts come out so clearly as in Murasaki Shikibu's 11th-century novel *The Tale of Genji*. Movies, *anime*, *manga*, music, paintings, poetry, plays, dance, novels, theater, and opera all have been inspired by its story and imagery. High school students commonly write essays about why *The Tale of Genji* forms the foundation of Japanese literature. When novelist Yasunari Kawabata gave his acceptance

---

3 Junichiro Tanizaki. *In Praise of Shadows*. Translated by Thomas J. Harper and Edward G. Seidensticker. (Vintage: London, 2001) 46.

speech for the Nobel Prize in Literature, he cited *The Tale of Genji* as "the highest pinnacle of Japanese literature. Even down to our day there has not been a piece of fiction to compare with it."[4]

Shikibu draws us into her world through the use of descriptive contrasts that we can easily visualize.

> "Their black hair, peeking beyond the hem of their gowns, vividly stood out against the white of the snow."[5]

> "Closed in ice,
> water between the rocks no longer goes,
> But the brilliantly lit moon
> freely through the sky flows."[6]

Black hair. White snow. Still water. Soaring moon. By masterfully placing one against another, Shikibu brings out hidden beauty beyond the people and

---

4 Yasunari Kawabata. *Japan, the Beautiful, and Myself.* Translated by Edward Seidensticker. (Tokyo: Kodansha International, 1981) 47.

5 Jakucho Setouchi. *The Tale of Genji.* Volume 4. Originally by Murasaki Shikibu. (Kodansha: Tokyo, 1997) 71. (English translation by author)

6 Ibid, 74.

objects themselves.

Kawabata clearly received his inspiration from *The Tale of Genji*, for his most famous novel, *Snow Country*, overflows with descriptions not unlike those found in it.

> "Shimamura glanced up at her, and immediately lowered his head. The white in the depths of the mirror was the snow, and floating in the middle of it were the woman's bright red cheeks. There was an indescribably fresh beauty in the contrast."[7]

He describes the beauty of this woman by contrasting her bright red cheeks against the whiteness of the snow. The snow somehow emphasizes the striking loveliness of the woman.

Japanese poetry and literature open my eyes to the incredible beauty of contrasts found in the gospel story. The All-Powerful as a helpless baby. The King of kings born in a barn. Light shining into darkness on that first Christmas night. The immortal become mortal. An innocent condemned as a criminal. The

---

7  Yasunari Kawabata. *Snow Country*. Translated by Edward G. Seidensticker. (New York: Vintage International, 1996) 48.

sinless taking on all sin. The unraveled woven together, strength out of weakness, victory from defeat.

In beholding the splendor of contrasts in the gospel of Christ, we cannot help but praise him.

1. What contrasts do you find particularly beautiful in nature?
2. What other contrasts are portrayed in the Bible that you find beautiful or meaningful?

# XIII.
## Ikebana and the Cross

> "Man, born of woman,
> few of days and full of trouble.
> Like a flower,
> he goes out and withers;
> and fleeing like a shadow,
> he does not stand."
> JOB 14:1–2 (literal translation by author)

**THE LINE STRETCHES ALL THE WAY** down the hall. Although more than a hundred people have been waiting with us for over an hour, no one seems to mind. A sense of anticipation and excitement fills the air. We all wait to enter Tokyo's Meguro Gajoen, the "elegant garden of Meguro," to see the works of a well-known master of *ikebana*, the traditional Japanese art

*Beauty inspires beauty.*

of flower arranging.

As I enter the exhibit, I marvel at the creativity of each display. Flowers and leaves, branches and bamboo, dirt, clay, and rocks combine in a seemingly endless variety of shapes and colors so different than the flower arrangements common in the States. The displays not only include flowers in full bloom but unopened bulbs, withered branches, and dead leaves. Rather than an abundance of flowers, they display a simple beauty with only a few flowers. The balance and contrasts of positive and negative space, abundance and austerity, life and death, permanence and impermanence, express a hidden beauty far beyond the objects themselves.

As I walk through the exhibit, I feel inspired to make something—to write a poem, paint a picture, or compose a piece of music. Beauty inspires beauty.

God created the many species of flowers, but he also created men and women with the imagination, creativity, and skill to arrange them. The beautiful variety of each work makes me mindful of the God of all creation, eternal and boundless, with no limits to his creativity.

The exhibit also makes me appreciate the short-lived charm of fleeting things. Here today, gone tomorrow, but this broken and dying world also aches for a glorious beauty that lasts forever.

> "All people are like grass, and all their glory is like the flowers of the field; the grass withers and the flowers fall, but the word of the LORD endures forever." (1 Peter 1:24–25)[1]

As I enjoy the fleeting beauty of *ikebana*, I cannot help but think of the paradoxical beauty of the cross—that gut-wrenching beauty of Jesus cut off from the land of the living. The enduring Word of the Lord withering and wilting on a tree. Jesus gave up his own brilliant glory to bring us into the "hope of glory" (Colossians 1:27). He lived a fleeting life and died so that we could flourish and live.

---

1 See also: "I am a rose of Sharon, a lily of the valleys" (Song of Songs 2:1). The speaker here is the bride of Solomon, and the Bible refers to Jesus as the bridegroom and his bride as the church. However, artists throughout Christian history have also referred to this rose as Christ: "*Crucified, laid behind a stone/You lived to die, rejected and alone/Like a rose, trampled on the ground/You took the fall and thought of me*" (Michael W. Smith, "Above All").

On the cross, we see the piercing contrast of life in death and the splendor of the timeless in the temporary. As in *ikebana*, the cross displays through brokenness a deeper and unexpected beauty that will never fade or fail.

1. What impression do you have of *ikebana* and flower arranging?
2. Do flowers bring you joy? What memories do you have of them?
3. What do you think about the beauty that comes through the fragility and transcience of flowers?

# XIV.
## *His Eye Is on the Sparrow*

"Are not five sparrows sold for two pennies?
Yet not one of them is forgotten by God."

LUKE 12:6–7

**ONE OF JAPAN'S GREATEST POETS,** Issa Kobayashi (1763–1827), frequently writes about the beauty he finds hidden in the small and unimportant.[1] To me, his poetry reads like wisdom literature in the Bible. Issa's very own name means "one tea," perhaps referring to one little broken tea leaf floating in a cup.

---

1 Kobayashi Issa's home was in Kashiwabara, which is now part of Shinanomachi, the nearest train station to Lake Nojiri. I think of Issa as a Japanese version of the American poet Emily Dickinson, who lived and wrote near where I grew up in Boston. Both Issa and Dickinson lived in obscurity, were incredibly prolific, and expressed a light-hearted joy in nature.

When I visited the Issa Memorial Museum in his hometown of Shinanomachi, a small green frog from one of his more popular poems guided me through his life.

やせ蛙 まけるな一茶 これにあり

*Scrawny frog*
*Hang in there*
*Issa is here*

Issa had great a love for creatures and objects that are overlooked by others, as he often showed in his poems. One of my favorites is about a small bird.

雀の子 そこのけそこのけ お馬が通る

*Baby sparrow*
*Get out of the way*
*A great horse comes through*

A majestic person and horse pass through town, but Issa gives all of his attention to a little sparrow he sees on the path.

Besides finding beauty in small things, Issa was

especially concerned for those suffering from the pain and loss of death, stemming from his own experiences at a young age. His mother passed away when he was only three years old. His grandmother then took care of him and passed away when he was 13. Then when he was a father, he lost one of his children. He captured the grief from that time this way:

露の世は　露の世ながら　さりながら

*The world is*
*Only a dewdrop.*
*And yet, and yet . . .*

The world may be like a dewdrop that disappears with the coming sun, yet Issa finds beauty, meaning, and value in life. He acknowledges the sadness, implied by the imagery of teardrops as dewdrops, while choosing not to give up.[2] When all three of Issa's

---

2 Another favorite poem of mine showing Issa's delight in a weak and fragile world include 花の陰　あかの他人は　なかりけり ("In the shadow of the blossoms, there are no strangers.") Cherry blossoms practically disappear in the first rain or wind. My first cherry blossom season in Japan lasted only two days, but their beauty brings us together. Another is 蝶とんで　我が身も塵の　たぐいかな ("Butterfly, fly! My body too is a kind of dust.") Dust surrounds the butterfly, but our bodies, too, are

children die at a young age, and then, so does his wife, he wrote:

<ruby>生<rt>い</rt></ruby>き<ruby>残<rt>のこ</rt></ruby>り　<ruby>生<rt>い</rt></ruby>き<ruby>残<rt>のこ</rt></ruby>りたる　<ruby>寒<rt>さむ</rt></ruby>さかな

*Outliving them*
*Outliving them all*
*Ah, the cold!*

This poem seems to foreshadow his own death: alone in an unheated barn in the middle of winter. That building still exists today. I often drive by it in the winter when my family goes to Nagano to ski. Issa's pain gave him great sympathy for the weak and grieving, while also leading him to bring life through humor, love, and creativity.

The attitude of Issa toward the weak especially makes me think of the attitude of Jesus.

> "Are not five sparrows sold for two pennies? Yet not one of them is forgotten by God. Indeed, the very hairs of your head are all numbered. Don't be afraid; you are worth more than many sparrows." (Luke

---

nothing but dust. Yet, we long to soar like the butterfly. The weakness of our dust does not determine our worth.

12:6–7)

Not one sparrow or one hair from our head goes unnoticed by God.[3] Insignificant things in the eyes of man have beauty, meaning, and worth. Jesus has sympathy and compassion for the weak and lowly.

> "A bruised reed he will not break, and a smoldering wick he will not snuff out." (Isaiah 42:3)

Though tempted to despair by the transience of life,[4] I have hope when I read the poetry of Issa. He shows us glimpses of the beauty that God imbues in the smallest things of this world.

---

3 Issa's poem makes me think of the chorus to "His Eye Is on the Sparrow" by Civilla D. Martin: "I sing because I'm broken, I sing because I'm free, For his eye is on the sparrow, and I know he watches me." A change from "happy" to "broken" was made in the lyrics by Megan Moody and sung by my friend September Penn at an event at Aoyama Gakuin University in Tokyo on December 18, 2017.

4 Harold Bolitho, *Bereavement and Consolation*. (New Haven: Yale University Press, 2003) 84.

1. What are examples of ephemeral and beautiful things in this world?
2. Where do you personally find hope in weakness?

# XV.
## *Plum Blossoms*

The word of the LORD came to me:
"What do you see, Jeremiah?"
"I see the branch
of an almond tree," I replied.
The LORD said to me,
"You have seen correctly,
for I am watching to see
that my word is fulfilled."
JEREMIAH 1:11–12

**JOSEPH "JO" HARDY NIIJIMA** (1843–1890) defied the strict national policy of isolationism in Japan when he boarded an American ship in 1864 and begged the ship captain to take him to the United States. Just a teenager when he arrived in Boston, a local wealthy family befriended him and paid for his schooling at Phillips Academy, Amherst College, and Andover Theological Seminary. He became the first-ever Japanese student to graduate from an American university and was also the first-ever Japanese Protestant pastor and evangelist.[1]

By the time he graduated, Niijima's home country had changed quite a bit. He could return to Japan openly as a Christian. He decided to establish a Christian university in Kyoto, the political and cultural heart of Japan, from which Christianity could spread throughout the nation.

The project entailed a lot more difficulty than he could have imagined. Hardly any Christians lived in Japan, so he found teachers almost non-existent. Money was hard to raise, and traditional laws made buying property very difficult. A friend remarked, "Establishing a Christian school in such a conservative traditional city is like commanding Mt. Hiei to jump

---

1 I feel particularly close to Niijima's story, because I grew up in the places around Boston where he lived. He even preached in my hometown of Lexington, Massachusetts. Also, like Niijima, I traveled from Boston to Japan as a missionary. I even played an organ concert in the chapel of Philips Academy, where Niijima went to school.

into Lake Biwa."[2] Mt. Hiei, the "mother mountain" of Buddhism in Japan, cast a long shadow over the city of Kyoto. An important temple established there in 788 A.D. powerfully influenced the training and spread of Buddhism.

One day while despairing over the unbelievable hurdles he had to face, Niijima saw a plum tree blooming in the snow. Encouraged, he took it as a sign that he stood at the very beginning of God's work in Japan. Plum trees bloom in the harshness of winter. Niijima wrote about this hope with the following poem.

似真理期梅
敢侵風雪開

*Truth is like the winter plum blossom*
*Daring to bloom in the wind and snow*

Back in the winter of 1597, the martyrdom of 26 Christians in Nagasaki started 250 years of heavy persecution in Japan. At that very same time, plum

---

2  Masao Takenaka, *When the Bamboo Bends*. (Geneva: WCC Publications, 2002) 7–8. The university he established is called Doshisha University.

blossoms began to bloom across the city. The flowers symbolized their hope that one day Christians would once again openly worship God. Those days reached fulfillment in Niijima's time, when Kyoto grew into one of the three early centers of Christianity, along with the cities of Sapporo and Kumamoto.

Hearing Nijima's story, I think about the very beginning of Jeremiah's ministry in the Bible. He lived during a very turbulent time leading into Babylonian captivity and the destruction of Jerusalem and the temple. He endured persecution throughout his life. He was ignored, ridiculed, and beaten (Jeremiah 20). People of his hometown even plotted to murder him (Jeremiah 11:18–20).

But at the very beginning of Jeremiah's ministry, God showed him an almond tree. In the Middle East, almond trees bloom first in the cold winter months. Just as almond trees watch for the coming of spring, God promised to watch through the coming hardship and adversity to see his promises fulfilled. The almond tree also represents the light of God's presence, for the golden lampstand in the tabernacle and temple was made to look exactly like the branches, buds, and blossoms of the almond tree (Exodus 25:31–36; 37:17–22).

When I see plum trees blossom in that transitional time between winter and spring, I remember the hope it symbolizes. I remember what it meant to Niijima, and what it continues to stand for today. We watch and wait, even in adversity, to see God's good promises fulfilled, and indeed receive glimpses of that even now.

1. What were big challenges of adversity and difficulty you had to overcome in your life?
2. In that situation, was there anything in particular that gave you hope?

# XVI.
## *Evergreen*

"I am like an evergreen tree."

HOSEA 14:8 (TLB)

**I SPEND A LOT OF TIME** in the mountains of Japan in the winter, when the green of the evergreens stands out in stark contrast to the white snow surrounding it. Though the wind blows, their leaves do not fall and are always green. No matter the temperature or the severity of the wind, their leaves seem to flourish with life.

A natural symbol of life, many people place evergreen trees and wreaths in their homes for Christmas. Christmas trees, originally called "paradise trees," symbolize the tree of life in both in the Garden of Eden and in the New Jerusalem.

Instead of trees and wreaths at Christmas, many Japanese decorate the front of their homes and buildings with *kadomatsu* or "gate pine." These decorations include bamboo and plum blossoms, the other "Three Friends of Winter" that anticipate the spring. Bamboo stalks sit at three different heights to represent heaven, earth, and man. When I see them, I am reminded of Christ, the sole reason that heaven and earth will reconnect one day.

God speaks through the prophet Hosea to compare himself to an evergreen, strong and full of life all year long.

> "I am like an evergreen tree, yielding my fruit to you throughout the year. My mercies never fail." (Hosea 14:8, TLB)

Whenever I see evergreen celebrated all around us as a sign of life and anticipation, I am once again reminded of how God gives these simple but poignant reminders of everlasting life.

1. What memories do you have related to Christmas trees or *kadomatsu*?
2. What is your image of evergreens?
3. What parts of creation show God as the source of life? What other examples can you think of besides evergreens?

# XVII.
## Onsen of Heavenly Rest

"My presence will go with you,
and I will give you rest."
EXODUS 33:14

**ONE OF THE MOST VOLCANIC** countries in the world, Japan is blessed with thousands upon thousands of naturally heated *onsen* hot springs. Steaming mineral-rich waters flow from beautiful mountainous landscapes, which heal both the body and the soul. Some of the best hot springs in the world can be found in Hakone, Atami, Kusatsu, and Beppu for their stunning views and extraordinary volumes of water.

My favorite *onsen* facilities are built with natural elements: walls of wood and bamboo rather than concrete, pathways of rocks and stones rather than tile, pools filled with waterfalls and streams rather than faucets. The sound of running water drowns out all cares and anxieties as it washes over me.

Nothing in Japan represents rest to most Japanese more than *onsen*, offering recovery from both physical and mental fatigue and stress. The hot water heals the muscles. Natural minerals heal the skin. Whether overworked, tired, sick, or in pain, these hot springs can bring relief. They provide a place to relax with family and friends without a thought to the passing of time. And nothing in Japan is perhaps closer to our state in the Garden of Eden or to the deep eternal rest that is promised to come.

> "The angel showed me the river of the water of life, as clear as crystal, flowing from the throne of God and of the Lamb." (Revelation 22:1)

What if the healing waters of the river of life are like the waters of an *onsen*? One day, will we sit in pools along this river completely washed and fully clean, as we delight in God, each other, and the world? On that day, we will certainly enjoy the perfect peace and healing that flows from the throne of Jesus.

> "Come to me, all you who are weary and burdened, and I will give you rest." (Matthew 11:28)

Jesus invites us to this place of rest and intimate community and, even now, the weary and burdened can begin to experience it.

True rest can only be found in heaven, but in the meantime, we can enjoy the many blessings of the Japanese *onsen*.

1. Have you ever been to a hot spring? What was it like?
2. What kind of situations do you find relaxing and peaceful?
3. What do you think the rest of heaven will be like?

# XVIII.
## Removing the Burden

Let us also lay aside every weight,
and sin which clings so closely . . .
looking to Jesus.
HEBREWS 12:1–2

**MY FAMILY AND I OFTEN STAY IN A CABIN**
in the mountains of Japan to get away from the city, be
surrounded by nature, breathe clean air, and rest both
the body and the soul.

However, one day makes me a bit nervous:
Garbage Day. Collection takes place from 7–8 AM,
Mondays and Fridays. I have to write my name in
large letters with permanent ink on the outside of
transparent bags so everyone can see the contents.
Wednesday recycling days are especially scary. Plastic

bottles, glass, aluminum, and steel need to be washed spotlessly and separated correctly. I only get one chance a week. With a failed inspection, I have to carry the rejected item back to the cabin.

Things I cannot throw away gradually accumulate in the corner of a room: an old rug, broken tools, a vacuum cleaner, empty paint cans, a broken suitcase, a bicycle. I cover them with old sheets trying to ignore their presence and smell, but they just get in the way.

One day, I hear a rumor about a garbage dump a short distance away. I immediately go look for it, but no one is there. All the doors are closed with no indication of operation hours.

After many trips, I finally find someone. I park my car and talk excitedly with the man inside to confirm I can dump that day before going back to get the trash. I hurriedly return, have the car weighed at the reception window, and receive a ticket. I enter cautiously and pull up to a large metal hole. As I throw in one piece of trash, I brace myself for an alarm or something to go off or for someone to start yelling in my direction. But nothing happens. *Is it really this easy?* I think to myself as I throw the rest of the garbage in. I cannot describe how refreshing it feels.

The car now empty and spacious with all the trash gone, I pay the fee at the reception window and leave. I timidly look back in the mirror to see if anyone follows, half-expecting sirens or red lights to stop me, but, again, nothing happens.

Through that experience, I felt released from the weight of sin and shame in the world. No matter how hard we try to deceive ourselves by hiding or ignoring it, broken relationships and memories of hurtful words continue to haunt us. Self-loathing and doubt follow us.

Jesus takes away all the burdens we cannot throw away. No matter the contents, he receives and pays for all our garbage. As we give each piece to Jesus, we come away with indescribable feelings of weightlessness and freedom.

Sadly, several years later that garbage dump shut down, and now the trash accumulates once again. But thankfully my burden of sin does not. Jesus stands ready to receive anything we want to give him. 24 hours a day, 7 days a week.

1. Is there any kind of garbage you would like to get rid of but do not know what to do with?

2. What would it feel like to have all the burdens of mistakes, sin, and shame removed forever?

# XIX.
## Silence of the Cross

He was oppressed and afflicted,

yet he did not open his mouth;

he was led like a lamb to the slaughter,

and as a sheep before its shearers is silent,

so he did not open his mouth.

ISAIAH 53:7

**HANDEL'S "HALLELUJAH" CHORUS** abounds with joy as melodies climb higher and higher, the orchestra plays faster and faster, and the singers repeat their chorus over and over. In the 1743 London premiere, the performance so moved King George II that he rose to his feet. Then, surprisingly, just before the climax, all the music stops. No one dares to move. A magnificent silence fills the hall, giving extraordinary power to a timpani-pounding grand finish.

In all classical music, composers write silence with as much attention as any note on a page. Performers, pipe organists in particular, calculate the release of every note as precisely as every attack. Because sound from the pipes does not fade away like on a piano, and pushing keys harder or softer does not make notes louder or softer, a skillful use of silence is crucial to keep the organ from feeling heavy and muddy. Rests form the very breath of the music.

In the book *Absolutely on Music*, Haruki Murakami records conversations with orchestra director Seiji Ozawa about various topics in music. I find it fascinating the way the two of them talk about the Japanese concept of *ma* (間), the space in-between, in relation to classical music.

*(In talking about Glenn Gould)*

OZAWA: "That's how you grab your audience and pull them in, isn't it? By skillfully placing the *ma* there, you have them. . . . Isn't that placement of *ma* amazing?"

*(In talking about Mitsuko Uchida)*

OZAWA: "And there, listen to the way she places that *ma*. This is the same passage where we heard Gould placing the *ma*."

MURAKAMI: "Now that you mention it, it is isn't it? The way she places that *ma* in the music . . ."[1]

As these two men discuss classical music, they refer to this Japanese concept of *ma* rather than silence. *Ma*, the space in between, holds a distinct beginning and end with more definition than just silence.

This "in between" space pervades Japanese art. *Pine Trees* by Hasegawa Tohaku clearly shows unpainted white space as important as strokes on the paper. In *ikebana* flower arranging, the negative space communicates as much as flowers and twigs. I think of *Noh* theater, where lack of movement expresses presence and strength. In *The Tale of Genji*, Murasaki

1 小澤征爾、村上春樹『小澤征爾さんと、音楽について話をする』(東京：新潮文庫、2014) 55, 89, 103. Author's translation from the Japanese. English published title: *Absolutely on Music: Conversations with Seiji Ozawa*.

Shikibu leaves the entire chapter "Vanished into the Clouds" with a completely blank page to express deep and heavy sorrow after Genji dies.

Sound and silence.

Movement and stillness.

Object and space.

Together, these things make me think of the silence of the cross. When Jesus suffered and hung on the cross, God was silent. When Jesus cried "Why?" with a loud voice, God did not answer. When Jesus breathed his last, a weighty negative space surrounded him without the presence of God. The perfect love they shared from eternity past . . . stopped.

Jesus's death brought the beginning of the greatest *ma* to ever pierce the world stage. The in-between space of the silence of God began with the cross and ended with the resurrection. The deafening silence of the cross shows the sacrificial love of God through that definitive time between Good Friday and Easter.

The good news of the gospel resounds through the ages through the silence of the cross.

1. When have you experienced a deep silence?

2. In what circumstances is the silence of 'ma' especially important?

3. What do you think about this comparison of '*ma*' in Japanese traditional arts to describe Jesus on the cross?

# XX.
## *God of the In-Between*

> There is one God
> and one mediator
> between God and mankind,
> the man Christ Jesus.
> 1 TIMOTHY 2:5

**I MAY NOT BE VERY GOOD AT IT,** but I like studying languages.[1] They drop me into worlds and cultures vastly different from my own.

While learning Japanese, I thought a lot about the character *ma* (間). Roughly translated as the space "in between," it does not have any English equivalent. The Japanese words for "human," "time," and "space" all

---

1 First printed by the Lutheran Society for Missiology. *Lutheran Mission Matters*, Volume XXV, No. 1 (Issue 50), May 2017, 97–104. Used by permission.

include this character. More specifically, the Japanese word for human is the "person in between" and the word for time is the "time in between." As I think more and more about the Japanese concept of *ma* and the "in between" of humanity, time, and space, I find far-reaching implications not only into a Japanese view of the world but glimpses into the depth of the gospel message.

## GOD OF THE "IN BETWEEN" OF HUMANITY

The Japanese word for "human"（人間）, pronounced *ningen*, combines the characters for "person" (人) and "in between" (間). Humanity, in its essence, consists of not only the "person" but also the relationship "in between" each person. This "in between" expresses identity as much as personality, gifts, and appearance, taking into account nurture as well as nature.

The character for "in between" (間) describes close relationships（仲間 , 間柄）(i.e., relationship to family and friends), society（世間）(i.e., relationship to community), civilian（民間）(i.e., relationship to nation), and many more. Relationships form a foundational part of our humanity and place in this world.

This significance of the "in between" relationships of humanity grows especially clear when they are broken.

> "The man and his wife . . . hid from the LORD God among the trees of the garden. But the LORD God called to the man, 'Where are you?' He answered, 'I heard You in the garden, and I was afraid . . . so I hid.'" (Genesis 3:8–10)

When mankind disobeyed God, the space "in between" God and man broke apart. Man became fearful and empty and experienced feelings of abandonment. "Your iniquities have separated you from your God" (Isaiah 59:2), wrote Isaiah. A gaping chasm opened up between God and humanity.

Like a falling row of dominoes, the relationships between people also broke. Humans descended into a state of semi-isolation, struggling to relate to each other in healthy and loving ways. Fighting increased. Danger, poverty, hunger, and discrimination entered the world.

*God the Son,*
*eternally existing*
*in a loving relationship*
*with God the Father,*
*was sent into this world*
*as the perfect "human"*
*to fulfill the "in between"*
*with God, people, and this earth.*

"While they were in the field, Cain attacked his brother Abel and killed him. Then the LORD said to Cain, 'Where is your brother Abel?' 'I don't know,' he replied. 'Am I my brother's keeper?'" (Genesis 4:8–9)

The relationship between humans and the earth fell apart as well.

"Cursed is the ground because of you." (Genesis 3:17)

Humans devolved from beautiful beings capable of taking care of the world to people at odds with everyone and everything. A vital part of God's creation disintegrated—the "in-between" of fellowship. In order to heal mankind, God had to restore the "in between" of humanity.

God the Son, existing eternally in a loving relationship with God the Father, was sent into this world as the perfect "human" (人) to fulfill the "in between" (間) with God, people, and this earth.

"The Word became 'a person' (人) and lived 'in between' (間) us." (John 1:14, author's translation from Japanese)

Jesus is that "person in between" who came down to fill the broken void and "bind everything together" (Colossians 3:14), because "in him all things hold together" (Colossians 1:17). The gospel message proclaims the salvation of mankind through the restoration of true love and intimacy.

> "'The virgin will conceive and give birth to a son, and they will call him Immanuel' (which means 'God with us')." (Matthew 1:23)

God who is "with us" is also "in between us." God comes to us relationally and restores the "in between" of humanity. He seeks us from the beginning of the Bible in Genesis when he asks, "Where are you?" to the end of the Bible in Revelation when he says, "I stand at the door and knock."

God persistently pursues an intimate relationship with us throughout human history. Jesus Christ now reigns as the Lord of our "in between"—the great Mediator in our relationships with God, each other, and this world.

## GOD OF THE "IN BETWEEN" OF SPACE

There are two places I recommend all my friends visit on their first trip to Tokyo: Meiji Shrine and Sensoji Temple. Meiji Shrine is the Shinto shrine dedicated to the Emperor Meiji, and Sensoji Temple is Tokyo's oldest Buddhist temple. Both of these places have taught me much about Japanese culture.

Trees, water, rocks, and expansive open spaces, "the empty in between" ( 空間 ), line the way to Meiji Shrine. Though located in the middle of the city, upon entering the path, one feels suddenly removed. A peaceful quiet fills the air. In contrast, the walk from the gate up to Sensoji Temple bustles with crowded shops selling food and souvenirs to noisy tourists, full of the energy of city life.

The two sites differ greatly but retain some things in common: a gate, a path, and a main building. The gate and main building are, of course, important, but the path "in between" also holds special meaning. I have only a superficial understanding of these things, but I can at least understand that the journey down the long path always plays an extremely beautiful and memorable part of the visit.

As a Christian, they make me think of Jesus's words, "I am the gate" (John 10:9) and "I am the way" (John 14:6). He also said, "'Destroy this temple, and I will raise it again in three days' . . . The temple he had spoken of was his body" (John 2:19–21). Jesus is the gate, the path, and the temple.

In my experience, American Christians tend to focus on goals—"at the gate" experiences of conversion or "at the temple" experiences of God's presence—more than "along the path" experiences. But consider various activities in Japan that follow a "path" or "way" (道), pronounced *dō* in Japanese: *jūdō* or The Way of Flexibility (柔道), *kendō* or The Way of the Sword (剣道), *kyūdō* or The Way of the Bow (弓道), *sadō* or The Way of Tea (茶道), *kadō* or The Way of Flowers (華道), and *shodō* or The Way of Writing (書道). They all involve slow and steady physical, emotional, and spiritual training.

I have been studying Shinkyokushinkai Karate with my boys for years now. I first started learning Shotokan Karate as a child when I was bullied in school and needed a way to protect myself. Since then, I have come to realize that there is much more to karate than self-defense.

The word *karatedō* ( 空手道 ) contains three very simple characters meaning "the way of the empty hand." This "way of the empty hand" shows me small truths about myself, a litmus test for my daily patterns. Are they balanced? Are they healthy? Karate keeps me aerobically fit and reduces stress in high-paced city life. It builds discipline and control over movement and anger. It builds flexibility to prevent serious injury. The way of the empty hand is a path to living more fully in this world.

Jesus called himself the way, the truth, and the life (John 14:6), so early Christians called themselves followers of "The Way."

> "There arose a great disturbance about the Way." (Acts 19:23)

> "I worship the God of our ancestors as a follower of the Way." (Acts 24:14)

What does it mean to be a follower of "The Way"?

Nothing we do can make us righteous in God's eyes. In weakness, we wander from God and stray to the left and to the right of the path.[2] The gospel does not just guide us along a path to follow but shows that Jesus is that path, the only way to God and his grace. The gospel does not show the path of the Christian life but affirms that Jesus already walked that path with perfect obedience for us.

Jesus is not only the gate and the temple, but he is also "The Way," the "space in between." In this space, we find joy and fulfillment. In this space, we find freedom and our spirits can dance. In this space, we have peace.

In the "space in between," we see Jesus. To be a follower of "The Way" means to live in the grace of God as fallen human beings in a fallen world. Rather than focusing only on the beginning or end of our journey, we recognize Jesus as that path we walk in the Christian life.

---

2  "Give careful thought to the paths for your feet and be steadfast in all your ways. Do not turn to the right or the left; keep your foot from evil." (Proverbs 4:26–27); "Whether you turn to the right or to the left, your ears will hear a voice behind you, saying, 'This is the way; walk in it.'" (Isaiah 30:21)

## GOD OF THE "IN BETWEEN" OF TIME

The Japanese word for time ( 時間 ) also makes me see the world and the gospel differently. It joins two characters meaning "a specific hour in telling time" (時) and the "in between" character *ma* (間). What does it mean to be "in between" time?

Humanity's first concept of time comes from the first day of creation when God made the night and the day.

> "There was evening, and there was morning—the first day." (Genesis 1:5)

We get our concept of the week from God's creation of the Sabbath, our concept of the month from God's creation of the orbit of the moon around the earth, and our concept of the year from God's creation of the orbit of the earth around the sun. Though mysterious in its implications, we also find the seasons in heaven through the tree of life, which "yields its fruit every month."

> "On each side of the river stood the tree of life, bearing twelve crops of fruit, yielding its fruit every

month." (Revelation 22:2)

Seasons have a huge influence on the Japanese view of time. Nobel Prize winner Yasunari Kawabata said in his acceptance speech, "We [Japanese] brush against and are awakened by the beauty of the four seasons."[3] Studies in the national and cultural identity of Japan point to the importance of the seasons. Writers of *haiku* and other poetry developed a formulaic use of seasonal words unlike neighboring countries in Asia.[4]

Japanese literature also often captures the importance and beauty of transitions in the seasons and from one time to another as seen in Sei Shonagon's opening to *The Pillow Book* from the tenth century.

> "In spring, the dawn—when the slowly paling mountain rim is tinged with red, and wisps of faintly crimson-purple cloud float in the sky."[5]

---

3  Yasunari Kawabata, *Japan, the Beautiful, and Myself*. Translated by Edward Seidensticker. (Kodansha International Ltd., 1968) 69.

4  Shuichi Kato, *Time and Space in Japanese Culture*. (Iwanami Shoten, 2007) 34.

5  Sei Shonagan, *The Pillow Book*. Translated by Meredith McKinney (Penguin Classics, 2007).

This sensitivity to time and transition shows up in the film *Your Name* by Makoto Shinkai, which artfully explores the "in between" of day and night, past and present, natural and supernatural. The fact that it became the highest-grossing *anime* movie of all time in Japan is proof that it resonates with Japanese people.

At some level, humans dwell in a constant state of "in between-ness." We always live in the midst of cycles. We wake, eat, work, play, and sleep in cycles. We breathe in and out in cycles, continuing the cycle God started with his first breath into us. Blood circulates through our arteries and veins. Cycles go all the way down to the cellular level, found even at the most foundational level of atoms. We are from dust and "to dust [we] will return" (Genesis 3:19).

Empress Jito expressed the beauty of "in between" transitions and cycles in a poem from the eighth century.

> "Spring seems to have passed into summer
> See the white silk robes spread to dry
> On the Mountain of Heavenly Perfume?"[6]

6  *Collection of Ten Thousand Leaves* (*Manyoshu*) I:28.

What season exists when spring is ending and summer is beginning? Either, neither, or both? Even though the temperature remains cool, we anticipate summer coming in this poetry through the washing and preparing of summer garments. We feel the ambiguity of time "in between" the seasons of spring and summer.

This sensitivity to the cycles of seasons in Japanese culture can even be found in the view of history. "Like the change of spring to summer to fall to winter, the flow of history is cyclical,"[7] writes Shuichi Kato. According to this scholar, history is cyclical, and people always move in the midst of these cycles. But we can also find this cyclical view of history in the Bible, especially in the history of Israel. Rescued from the bondage of slavery in Egypt, Israel returned to the Promised Land (after enduring forty years of "in-between" wandering in the desert) only to be captured and forced into slavery again by the nations of Assyria, Babylon, and other nations. Cycles of rebellion against

---

7  Shuichi Kato,『日本文化における時間と空間』(*Time and Space in Japan*), Tokyo: Kodansha, 2016, p. 34. Translated by author.

God, repentance, and salvation repeat over and over.

Yet, through these cycles of rebellion, repentance, and redemption, the people of Israel learned dependence on God. God redeems the destructive elements of the cycle for our good.

The Christian life constantly moves through cycles of sin, repentance, forgiveness, and renewal in the gospel. After salvation, we fail. No matter how deep our understanding of the gospel, we cannot move forward in a perfect linear path of sanctification. We inevitably follow this cycle and experience the grace of God over and over again.

We live in the already-but-not-yet of God's promises, waiting for the complete renewal and redemption of mankind. We linger as an "in-between" people longing for everything to be made right.

> "The whole creation has been groaning as in the pains of childbirth right up to the present time. Not only so, but we ourselves, who have the firstfruits of the Spirit, groan inwardly as we wait eagerly for our adoption to sonship, the redemption of our bodies." (Romans 8:22–23)

*We wander in the
already-but-not-yet of God's promises,
waiting for the complete renewal
and redemption of mankind.
We grapple with life
as "in between" people longing
for everything to be made right.*

We wander in the already-but-not-yet of God's promises, waiting for the complete renewal and redemption of mankind. We grapple with life as "in-between" people longing for everything to be made right.

When the pain of the "not yet" leads us to Jesus, we realize he stands as the great "in between" mediator of God and man, the crux of creation, the hero who knows suffering.

Jesus wept at the tomb of Lazarus and said, "My time has not yet come," at the wedding in Cana. Jesus expressed his frustration at the brokenness of this world when he said, "Jerusalem, Jerusalem . . . How often have I longed to gather your children together, as a hen gathers her chicks under her wings" (Matthew 23:37). On the cross, Jesus said, "It is finished!" but everything broken is not yet fixed.

We live in Holy Saturday, between the suffering and death of Good Friday and the joy of the resurrection on Easter Sunday. The cross gives immeasurable meaning to our present "groaning" as we look forward to the new creation.

Amidst all the healthy and destructive and "in

*We live in Holy Saturday,*
*between the suffering and death*
*of Good Friday*
*and the joy of the resurrection*
*on Easter Sunday.*

between" cycles of this yet-broken life, God remains the one and only "still point of the turning world."[8] On earth and in heaven, we are dependent on God alone for salvation and true rest. The resurrection alone proves that all God's promises will one day be fulfilled and that he indeed reigns as God over all time, including the time "in between."

Languishing in all the cycles and ambiguities between one time and another, we can only rely on the unchanging God who "is the same yesterday, today, and tomorrow" (Hebrews 13:8) and reside in his promises.

## CONCLUSION

The Japanese concept of *ma* opens my eyes in a new way to the God of the Bible. The Alpha and the Omega, the beginning and the end, God also inhabits everything "in between." The goal of our faith is not simply to save our souls at one particular point in time but to live now and forever in his grace.

God of the humanity "in between" restores our relationships through love.

---

8  T. S. Eliot, "Burnt Norton" from *Four Quartets*. 1935.

God of the space "in between" connects us to himself by his grace.

God of the time "in between" soaks our hearts in his promises as we live in the past, present, and future of our earthly lives.

May God renew our praise daily as we absorb this gospel hope offered to us even more deeply through the art and culture of every language, tribe, and nation.

1. Do you think this Japanese concept of the "in between" is essential to what it means to be human?

2. Do you think the process of getting somewhere is as important as the destination?

3. Do you think humans live in the "in between" ( 間 ) of time ( 時間 ), in a constant state of "in between-ness"?

4. In what way does the concept of "in between" help you understand the gospel more deeply?

# Acknowledgments

Since my arrival in Japan, I have developed close friendships with many. Besides the great experiences we've had together, we have also often talked about the hidden beauty of Japan. Through these friends, I have learned much about this world and the beauty and grace of God. This little book was birthed out of those times together. I would especially like to thank Kei, Hitomi, Hiro, Mona, and Peter, whose names are already mentioned in the book. I would also like to thank more people than I can possibly list here, everyone part of the community that has so readily accepted my family into their lives. God bless you all.

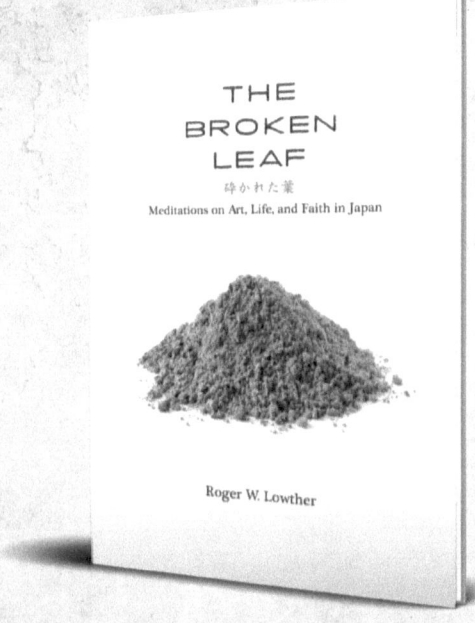

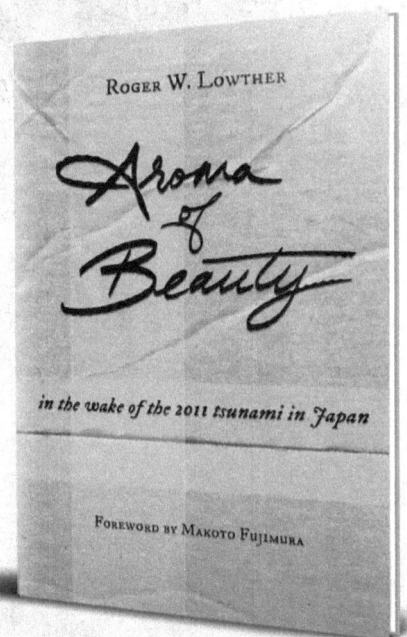

# Feedback

Thank you for reading *Hidden Beauty*. Would you take a moment to share your thoughts on this book by leaving a review on Amazon and Goodreads? This is not only a huge help to me but gives others a sense of what this book is about.

- Go to this book on my Amazon author page: *amazon.com/author/rogerlowther*
- Hover over the Amazon ratings and click on "See all customer reviews."
- Click on "Write a customer review."

You can also connect with me directly through my website *www.rogerwlowther.com* or sign up for newsletters to receive more stories from Japan and updates on other writing and recording projects.

I look forward to hearing from you.

Photo: Rebecca Robinson

**ROGER W. LOWTHER** is the founder and director of Community Arts Tokyo, director of Faith & Art at Grace City Church Tokyo, and coordinator for the MAKE Collective, a global network of artists working in foreign missions. He has been serving with Mission to the World in Japan since 2005. Roger has studied at The Juilliard School, Columbia University, and Reformed Theological Seminary.

Roger has won numerous competitions as a pipe organist and released five albums. Roger has also authored *The Broken Leaf* (2019), *Pippy the Piano and the Very Big Wave* (2020), *Aroma of Beauty* (2021), and *A Taste of Grace* (2024). He lives in downtown Tokyo with his wife Abi and children.

*www.rogerwlowther.com*

www.ingramcontent.com/pod-product-compliance
Lightning Source LLC
Chambersburg PA
CBHW031531120626
46545CB00005B/2093